Companion to Becoming Magdalene

Journaling and Shared Group Discussion

a spiritual exercises guidebook

Jennifer Ristine

En Route Books and Media, LLC

Saint Louis, MO

⊕ENROUTE
Make the time

En Route Books and Media, LLC
5705 Rhodes Avenue
St. Louis, MO 63109

Cover credit: Jennifer Ristine
Copyright © 2025 Jennifer Ristine

ISBN-13: 979-8-88870-440-0
Library of Congress Control Number:
Available at https://catalog.loc.gov

Table of Contents

PART ONE: Principle & Foundation

Called to Love

We love because God loved us first.
1 John 4:19

Corresponds to Prologue – Chapter 6

Spiritual Exercises' Dynamic (Part 1)
Principle & Foundation
Read the following before Becoming Magdalene Prologue

Begin with the big picture. God Loves You! In Part One we will explore the movements of the soul in the principal and foundation of spiritual exercises. We contemplate the desires of God's heart through his Original Plan by considering His creative work in the world and His providential care for us. In the light of His unconditional love, we discover our identity as His beloved children. Immersed in this truth, we marvel that all is gift.

In the principle and foundation, we receive an invitation to turn to our Papa God, as Saint Therese of Lisieux once expressed. God offers us a path toward "innocence," a purity of heart, free of whatever enslaves us. We are invited to desire and believe in the possibility of a state in which God truly reigns supreme and is glorified by our lives dedicated to Him. If this aspiration exists, it is because God has loved us first. He made us for loving communion, with Him above all else, and then, all else in and through Him.

Saint Ignatius of Loyola suggests that the retreatant begin with the end in mind. In one of the first numbers of his *Spiritual Exercises* he reminds us that we are created for something more! To "praise, reverence, and serve God our Lord, and by this means to save his soul".[i] All creation is good and can serve toward this goal, depending on our relationship with God's gifts.

God's revelation speaks the truth about who we are and why we exist. We are created to love and be loved. But many times, life circumstances and choices obscure this truth, distorting the echo of God's call. Nonetheless, the Lord persistently tugs at our hearts, hoping we will see and hear anew. He meets us precisely where we are. Paradoxically, a struggle begins. A tension results, making the truth of God's Love even more pronounced. He calls us to new life.

In the first chapters, we set the stage, visiting important memories and the echo of God's call in Mary's heart to love and be loved. Created by Love, she is restless for her true home. She senses that she belongs to something and Someone beyond herself, beyond even what the world has offered her so far. Created for love, she seeks to make sense of past relationships and she longs for purpose. Having grown up in an educated Jewish household she recalls God's Word that contradicts her subjective and distorted sense of self. The seeds of truth strive to grow through the weeds of oppressive lies that attempt to choke out the barely visible life. No matter the tension, her heart resonated with the echo of God's Original Plan for her life. An existential restlessness takes hold. She knows she is made for something more.

Mary is, of course, the central character, but the hero of the story is Jesus. You won't see him yet, but he is there, unseen, like in our own lives. The entire story is told by an old friend who opens the scene in a garden, echoing a scriptural beginning when man and woman walked in friendship with God. Perhaps that place feels disconcerting at first. But soon we recognize it as a realm of interior intimacy, truth and decision, a place we know in the depth of our hearts. It is the space of a life-giving encounter, for which we long and where we belong.

Read from the Prologue to Chapter 6.

Reflection & Prayer (Part 1)
Reflect after Reading Prologue to Chapter 6

We have glimpsed into various wounds of Mary's past and the tumultuous state of her present. An existential tension shakes her to the core. She examines her life in the light of a Creator God and asks fundamental questions. Who is this God I once believed in as a child? Is He truly good and sovereign over all things? Over my life? Why do I exist? Do I have a purpose and where do I belong? At the heart of her restlessness lies a profound longing to love and be loved. She grapples with the truth of her fundamental dignity of being made in God's image and likeness. She wrestles with affective memories, born from life circumstances, choices, and relationships. They threaten to obscure her true vision of reality. Revelation, from her memory of God's Word, nourishes hope while clashing with her false image of God and self. Apply her interior experiences to your own.

SACRED SCRIPTURE

Take note of predominant scriptural passages that moved you. What word or phrase resonated more than any other? What predominant interior movements were provoked as you read them? Did you sense a strengthening in faith, hope or charity? Consider those passages as consoling and strengthening experiences. Return in prayer to those that strengthened you.

Scripture Passage	Phrase or Word	Interior Movements (predominant feeling, resonance or impulse)	Strengthening of faith, hope or love for God?

LIFE EXPERIENCES

Take note of any of Mary Magdalene's experiences, be they interior and emotional or exterior and historical, that moved you. How do you identify with her? What predominant memories and emotions from your own life were provoked? Take those moments to prayer, asking for light to see where and how God was present and acting. How was the Lord inviting you to greater faith, hope, love?

Mary's experience	Interior Movements (predominant feeling, resonance or impulse)	Memories of my life

SPIRITUAL LIFE MAP

Use the Spiritual Life Map charts at the end of the *Companion* to take note of the PEOPLE & EVENTS in your life that have shaped the perception of your identity and purpose, and your perception of God. Continue to add to your list as you work your way through *Becoming Magdalene*.

TAKE TIME TO PRAY!

The following prayer exercises may help you to enter into the spiritual dynamic of the Principle & Foundation.

- ♥ Invite the Holy Spirit into your prayer. Make an act of faith and trust that the Lord is present and that He desires to be with you.
- ♥ Read Genesis 1:26-31 and 2:7-9.
- ♥ Imagine God, Creator of the universe, creating all things from nothing…*out of love, for you.*
- ♥ Imagine God breathing life into you.
- ♥ Imagine God, Father of all the living, placing you in the center of the garden of paradise.
- ♥ Imagine walking, hand in hand with the Lord, your God.
- ♥ Ask Him why He created you? And listen.
- ♥ What is that like? What is your heart moved to ask, say or do?
- ♥ Close with an act of loving reverence and gratitude that He has created you in His image and likeness, out of pure gratuitous love. Or continue as you felt moved to pray.

PART TWO: First Week (1)

Called to Life

Remember, Lord, your great mercy and love,
for they are from of old.
Do not remember the sins of my youth
and my rebellious ways;
according to your love remember me,
for you, Lord, are good.
Psalm 25:6-7

Corresponds to Chapters 7-9

Spiritual Exercises' Dynamic (Part 2)
First Week (1)
Read the following before Becoming Magdalene (Chapter 7-9)

The "Principle and Foundation" of spiritual exercises grounds us in the conviction of God's love as manifested through his creative action in the world. Awe and reverence prevail before the providential goodness of God, Father and Creator. He offers us a privileged participation in His Love, using His gifts of creation to return to Him. But face to Love, we fall short. Our response may be weak or resistant. Disordered tendencies give away the reality of our inescapable, sinful, human condition. We abuse our God-given freedom, as Adam and Eve once did. The remedy? Accept the true narrative of our lives: God's merciful love reaches into the depths of our misery. Jesus himself steps into the messiness of our human situation.

Saint Ignatius invites us to contemplate this reality in a series of meditation within "The First Week". Consider the consequences of sin, original and personal, and the fall of Adam, Eve and the angels. Meditate on the eschatological mysteries of our faith: death, judgment, heaven and hell. Far from self-condemnation, a predominant thread of mercy weaves together the fragments of our lives in the light of time and eternity. The Father's merciful love, through the gift of his Son, emerges, creating a hopeful image of what we are called to - we are called to life. Through this redemptive lens, conversion gains a foothold and we find ourselves with the "space" to sincerely repent in freedom and love, rather than live in fear.

In the "first week", Mary Magdalene faces her demons. Enter the tension she experienced. Life hangs in the balance. The Lord desires to set her free of the demons, or idols, that enslave her. Like her, we wrestle with attachments of the heart. We create our own idols. The heart deviates and becomes blind to truth. We must uncover the lies obscuring our true identity and vocation which keep us holding fast to false securities, be they in the form of our self-image, concepts of God, patterns of destructive behavior, or material objects.

Ask for the grace to see clearly. What idols are planted in your heart in place of the Lord? You are not alone. We all have them. They are rooted in ego-centric tendencies. Discover how you wrestle between life and death, between senselessly holding on and courageously letting go in order to assent to God's triumph within. Notice any wrestling takes place in the depths of your interior. What stirs within? We call these interior movements of the heart, be they resistance, spiritual consolation, or spiritual desolation. A spiritual director can be of great help here. At the source is God, the evil spirits, and our human spirit. It is not always black and white. God offers us life. Evil spirits attempt to lead us toward death. And our own psychology may be steeped in false convictions about ourselves, God and reality.

As a simple rule of thumb, be aware of where the heart tends. Do you detect inclinations toward vulnerability, welcoming God's presence and action? Or tendencies to close one's self to God, hiding in shame like Adam and Eve? Is the Lord consoling by strengthening your faith, hope or love? Toward living in the "naked truth" before His gaze? Or do you tend to despair and flight from the truth of self and God? Listen and accompany Mary Magdalene as she begins to notice the movements within her own heart. *Read Chapters 7-9.*

Reflection & Prayer (Part 2)
First Week (1)
After Reading Chapters 7-9

SACRED SCRIPTURE

Take note of predominant scriptural passages that moved you. What word or phrase resonated more than any other? What predominant interior movements (feeling, resonance, impulse, inclination, virtue/vice, thoughts) were provoked as you read them? Did you sense a strengthening in faith, hope or charity? Consider those passages as consoling and strengthening experiences. Return in prayer to those that strengthened you.

Scripture Passage	Phrase or Word	Interior Movements	Strengthening of faith, hope or love for God?

LIFE EXPERIENCES

Take note of any of Mary Magdalene's experiences, be they interior and emotional or exterior and historical, that moved you. How do you identify with her? What predominant memories and emotions from your own life were provoked?

Mary's experience	Interior Movements	Memories of my life

SPIRITUAL LIFE MAP

Continue to add to your list as you work your way through *Becoming Magdalene.*

NAME THE PREDOMINANT MOVEMENTS

Can you recognize the predominant movements described in Mary Magdalene's experience? Now examine your own life right now. What are the predominant movements that you experience?

✓ Thoughts or movements of the heart (affective movements) that engender hope and trust in a merciful God?

✓ Thoughts or movements of the heart that engender despair, despondency and distrust of a provident God?

✓ Tension between what you felt was a deeper call to conversion and the temptation to remain where you are, in a state that is not life-giving?

✓ Interior temptations and "voices" that tell you lies about your dignity despite your personal falls? The "voices of the enemy" trying to gain ground, condemning you? Name them.

✓ The nudging or impulses of hope and confidence in a merciful God? The voice of the Lord ("nudges", impulses, inspirations, interior "movements of the heart") encouraging you or lifting you up, nurturing courage to repent, or patience to endure, or faith, hope and charity?

✓ Can you name the fears and their accompanying thoughts that paralyze you or seem to hold you back or resist turning to the Lord in greater faith and trust?

PART THREE: First Week (2)

Called by Mercy

But because of his great love for us,
God, who is rich in mercy,
made us alive with Christ
even when we were dead in transgressions—
it is by grace you have been saved.
Ephesians 2:4-5

Corresponds to Chapters 10-14

Spiritual Exercises' Dynamic (Part 3)
First Week (2)

Read before Becoming Magdalene (Chapter 10-14)

We continue reflecting on the themes from the First Week of Ignatius' Spiritual Exercises. He sets up the human situation and reveals what is at stake: life or death, freedom or slavery. What will we choose? Better said, *who* will we follow? The challenge is to examine one's life in the proper way, within the context of salvation history. Far from a moralistic rigidness that focuses only on one's sin, we are encouraged to contemplate the whole truth in the light of God's merciful love. From this Christian cosmo-vision, we may experience the courage to be vulnerable, fight the good fight, and accept the hand of God stretched out to us.

The bible, from Genesis to Revelation, testifies to the cosmic war fought to establish God's Kingdom against the tidal wave of idols that threaten the life of God's people. Likewise, a battle wages in every human heart. It's a cosmic battle between good and evil, life and death. While the war has been won through the Paschal mystery of Jesus Christ, the human heart remains the climactic battleground where victory is applied or rejected. Hence, the drama plays out in the arena of human freedom, perplexingly resistant to God's conquest. But rest assured. The Lord does all he can to woo us into receiving his gift of life. It is his way of mercy.

A soul that is bound in unfreedom may find it difficult to identify God's wooing versus the lure of the evil one. So mercy's hand comes in many forms. Illuminations of light could strike fear into our souls as it did for Saul, who eventually became St Paul. Friends or relatives could express concern for our well-being, leading us to a sincere examination of conscience and disposition of humility necessary for conversion. Or a momentary grace touches us as a gaze of mercy, inviting us to receive forgiveness and healing. It's as though God creates a sliver of space, a momentary respite or clarity, where we can freely hold out our arms and welcome His patient and persistent presence. Let's contemplate God's "wooing" revealed in the movements of Mary Magdalene's heart. She must come to a place of truth where fear gives way to vulnerability, opening a path to liberation and greater freedom.

Read Chapters 10-14.

Reflection & Prayer (Part 3)

First Week (2)

After Reading Chapters 10-14

SACRED SCRIPTURE

Take note of predominant scriptural passages that moved you. What word or phrase resonated more than any other? What predominant interior movements were provoked as you read them? Did you sense a strengthening in faith, hope or charity? Consider those passages as consoling and strengthening experiences. Return in prayer to those that strengthened you.

Scripture Passage	Phrase or Word	Interior Movements	Strengthening of faith, hope or love for God?

LIFE EXPERIENCES

Take note of any of Mary Magdalene's experiences, be they interior and emotional or exterior and historical, that moved you. How do you identify with her? What predominant memories and emotions from your own life were provoked?

Mary's experience	Interior Movements	Memories of my life

SPIRITUAL LIFE MAP

Continue to add to your list as you work your way through *Becoming Magdalene.*

QUESTIONS FOR JOURNALING OR SHARING

If you were to examine your life (examination of conscience) today, under whose gaze would you be: the gaze of Jesus? the gaze of the world with its standards? the gaze of the "enemy of our soul" who wants you to flee from the possibility of encountering the merciful God?

Have any of the following helped you to draw nearer to the Lord, experience the love of God, or provoked clarity about your life or conversion?
- ✓ *True concern from someone, with no hidden meaning or agenda behind their empathy?*
- ✓ *The Word of God?*
- ✓ *A homily or sermon?*
- ✓ *A confrontation with a loved one?*

How do you sense that God looks upon you? With kindness, tenderness and mercy? In judgment and wrath? With expectation, firmness or encouragement? How does your perception of God's gaze upon you affect your willingness to be in His presence?

Have you experienced the merciful embrace of God? What do you find most challenging about receiving this?

TAKE TIME TO PRAY!

The following prayer exercises may help you to enter into the spiritual dynamic of the First Week.[ii]

- ♥ Invite the Holy Spirit into your prayer. Make an act of faith and trust that the Lord is present and that He desires to be with you.

- ♥ Ignatius recommends the following preparatory prayer: Lord God, grant that all my intentions, actions and operations may be directed purely to the service and praise of Your Divine Majesty.[iii]

- ♥ Read Genesis 3:1-15 on the fall of our first parents. Prayerfully enter the scene, as though entering your own memory of the event.

- ♥ Consider how the Lord sets up the parameters of their freedom out of love and concern for their well-being in the present moment. What do you feel before, during and after they choose to disobey God's warning?

- ♥ Prayerfully consider moments in your life when you sought security in the creations of God versus the Lord Himself, setting up idols in your heart other than the Lord.

- ♥ Imagine the Creator of the world coming as man to save you personally from all the consequences of sin, both inherited and personal sin.

- ♥ If you have a crucifix, offer a prayer, as to a friend, in a spirit of reverent gratitude and praise, and ask him what you can do for him.

- ♥ Consider encountering the Lord in the sacrament of mercy (confession) in order to bring your idols before him. Let his love and mercy destroy them, offering you new life.

Conclusion to Principle and Foundation and the First Week
God's Loving Initiative & Our Response

Pondering Mary Magdalene's interior journey teaches us a beautiful truth: God always takes the initiative and finds ways to speak to the human heart. He loves us, "nudges us" to take a step toward Him, and awaits our response. The longings of our hearts can be tell-tale signs of God's action in our lives. No matter where we are, the Lord comes to meet us. He looks for a little crack in our façade and finds his way in. Perhaps the open door is a memory of times past of a simple child-like relationship with God, inviting a return to simple trust in a loving Father. Perhaps it is a cry out to the Lord in the deeply felt need for a redeemer, inviting a spirit of repentance or dependence on His mercy. The open door could be the sacred memory of God's providential action throughout history as revealed in the pages of sacred scriptures, inviting praise and confidence. It could be a recognition of the blessings received, inviting confidence in God's fidelity. Finally, the open door may be a profound experience of solitude that converts to welcoming the Lord's coming as friend, companion, consoler, or sweet guest of the soul.

No matter where we are, God seeks to draw near, appealing to our deeply rooted need for him. He is the potter described in Jeremiah 18:1-16. We are like clay in his hands. Through Jeremiah, God revealed his desire that his people turn back to him and receive His life. They had the power to preserve or destroy it. God desires to give life. In Jesus' words, "A thief comes only to steal and slaughter and destroy; I came so that they might have life and have it more abundantly".[iv]

He not only gives us physical, biological life, but invites us to enter into the mystery of his own life, where we participate in his providential plan. "For I know well the plans I have in mind for you—oracle of the Lord—plans for your welfare and not for woe, so as to give you a future of hope"[v]. What a mysterious gift!

Life's busy activities, the background music of our own concerns, the punches that life throws us, and our own selfish gropings, threaten our attentiveness to the original call that echoes within us. Listen to that existential tension. It is the call to life and love. The Lord wants to remind us who he is for us and who we are for Him. He calls us in the midst of our "revelries". He flashes before our eyes the great dignity to which we have been called. It is a dignity we already possess as his creation, as images of His Son, and as beloved children. We must simply live in this truth! Let us give thanks and sing the marvel of God's love with the prayer of the Psalmist:

When I see your heavens, the work of your fingers, the moon and stars that you set in place— What is man that you are mindful of him, and a son of man that you care for him? Yet you have made him little less than a god, crowned him with glory and honor. You have given him rule over the works of your hands, put all things at his feet: All sheep and oxen, even the beasts of the field, the birds of the air, the fish of the sea and whatever swims the paths of the seas. O Lord, our Lord, how awesome is your name through all the earth![vi]

PART FOUR: Second Week (1)

Called to Friendship

Put on then, as God's chosen ones, holy and beloved, heartfelt compassion, kindness, humility, gentleness, and patience, bearing with one another and forgiving one another, if one has a grievance against another; as the Lord has forgiven you, so must you also do. And over all these put on love, that is, the bond of perfection.
Colossians 3:12-14

Corresponds to Chapters 15-22

Second Week (1)

Read before Becoming Magdalene (Chapter 15-22)

Mercy met misery. Now Mary Magdalene is anxious in a different way. It is a fresh beginning. Time for a new venture. The blessing of new life ushers in an initial zeal to follow Jesus. Mary Magdalene, the new woman in Christ, walks forward in consolation. But a naïve self-confidence in her recently found freedom may be overestimated. She will be alarmed when engrained egocentric habits continue to manifest themselves and old patterns of attachments resurface. Repentance is not the end of the story, nor is the decision to follow Jesus. We, like Mary Magdalene, "accompany Jesus around Galilee."

St Ignatius' Second Week invites us to walk with Jesus in prayerful contemplation of his person, his teachings, and healings. The fruit we desire is to know the Lord more profoundly so as to love him more passionately and follow him more faithfully. Ask for an interior knowledge, to know his words, thoughts, feelings, desires. And to know him from within ourselves. In this process we discover a personal friend. He is someone with whom we want to walk through life. Far from a romantic ideal, it provokes an ongoing transformation. What does "accompanying Jesus around Galilee" look like?

Galilee is a paradoxical place of beauty and purification. The incredibly hot months turn hillsides into an ugly, dry, and barren looking countryside. But wait...that passes. The chilly winter rains replenish the apparently barren soil. Lush greenery creeps its way through the dead brush. Patience for spring wins viewers the reward of splendid scenes of colors when purple, yellow, and red wildflowers splatter the hilly landscapes with their brilliance.

Periods of dryness purify the soul. Periods of rain make way for the germination of God's seed of grace. And periods of sun give birth to the flowers of virtue. The dynamic of our cooperative dance with God's love and mercy continues as friendship with Jesus blossoms. This is our life with the Lord. Relationships take time, effort, patience, reciprocation, listening. We accompany Jesus and let him accompany us. In this process, we may feel we are sliding backwards, then moving forward, ascending ever higher and falling deeper. Surprises abound. We are surprised at our continued weaknesses. Astonished when we experience a strength not our own. Flabbergasted by new manifestations of egotism. And yet delighted when we discover that we have truly fallen in love with the Lord. Let's watch Mary as she continues an ever-deeper conversion from the "old woman" to the "new woman." Watch and learn as she begins her walk with the Lord.

Read Chapters 15 -22.

Reflection & Prayer (Part 4)

After Reading Chapters 15-22

SACRED SCRIPTURE

Take note of predominant scriptural passages that moved you. What word or phrase resonated more than any other? What predominant interior movements were present as you read them? Did you sense a strengthening in faith, hope or charity? Consider those passages as consoling and strengthening experiences. Return in prayer to those that strengthened you.

Scripture Passage	Phrase or Word	Interior Movements	Strengthening of faith, hope or love for God?

LIFE EXPERIENCES

Take note of any of Mary Magdalene's experiences, be they interior and emotional or exterior and historical, that moved you. How do you identify with her? What predominant memories and emotions from your own life were provoked?

Mary's experience	Interior Movements	Memories of my life

SPIRITUAL LIFE MAP

Use the Spiritual Life Map charts at the end of the *Companion* to take note of the PEOPLE & EVENTS in your life that have shaped your perception of your identity and purpose, and your perception of God. Continue to add to your list as you work your way through *Becoming Magdalene*.

QUESTIONS FOR JOURNALING OR SHARING

Who is Jesus for you? In your walk with Jesus, what have you come to discover about him? What most attracts you? Is there a particular passage or image in which he comes alive for you? Write a brief prayer to Jesus, praising and thanking him for how he has revealed himself to you.

TAKE TIME TO PRAY!

The following prayer exercise may help you to enter into the spiritual dynamic of the Second Week.[vii]

- ♥ Invite the Holy Spirit into your prayer. Make an act of faith and trust that the Lord is present and that He desires to be with you.

- ♥ Ignatius recommends the following preparatory prayer: Lord God, grant that all my intentions, actions and operations may be directed purely to the service and praise of Your Divine Majesty.[viii]

- ♥ Ask for the grace to be attentive to the Lord's call, and magnanimity and diligence to respond.

- ♥ Imagine someone whom you look up to, be they a famous leader, media influencer, parent or a close friend. That person invites many people to join in a great and noble project of importance and wide influence, doing good for many people and of which you long to play a part. You have dreamt of being able to do such a project but never knew how it would be possible. Now you see it is possible with their leadership. But it will imply much sacrifice of time, applying your talents, and perhaps foregoing some of your personal treasures.

- ♥ Now consider an even more worthy project, one of eternal consequence. Your leader is Christ your Lord, Eternal King. Listen to his invitation. "I wish to conquer all hearts for my heavenly Kingdom and for my Father. If you wish to join me, take up your cross and follow me, because those who follow me in suffering, will also follow me in glory."

- ♥ Ask him what this cross may be? What must be "left behind"? Pride, comforts, vain pursuits, unhealthy and bad habits, etc? What must be endured? The judgments of others as you live as a Christian, the sacrifice implied by commitments that nurture your faith in Jesus?

- ♥ Desiring to follow the Lord, offer an act of trust and oblation.[ix] Write your own or pray:
My Lord and my God, Father, Son and Holy Spirit, I come before you and surrender all to you in the presence of your heavenly court with the angels, saints and my Mother. Grant me courage and determination to follow and serve you, so you may extend your Kingdom in my heart, in my family, and in the people with whom I interact daily. I praise, adore, and thank you!

PART FIVE: Second Week (2)

Called to Conviction

Now faith is the assurance of things hoped for,
the conviction of things not seen.
Hebrews 11:1

Corresponds to Chapters 23-30

Spiritual Exercises' Dynamic (Part 5)
Second Week (2)

Read before Becoming Magdalene (Chapter 23-30)

Mary Magdalene sought to reciprocate the love she experienced by offering resources from her own livelihood. But nothing measures up to the gratuity of the gift received. Her gratitude, coupled with this awareness, is a first step of humility. When she finally resolves to follow Jesus, her initial enthusiasm is tempered with a harsh reality check. She wants to befriend Jesus, but her new venture rubs against her ingrained patterns of thinking, feeling, and acting. The old woman still writhes from within, attempting to assert itself in her new reality.

Mary frequently found herself at crossroads, in which she faced a choice: follow Jesus or return to her former ways, not only in her external following, but in the depth of her heart where habitual ways of thinking, feeling and acting were formed, convictions grew, and life-defining decisions were fashioned. The decision, to be mature, must be conscious, intentional, and freely made.

The rough road of "becoming" that which Our Lord calls us to be is a precious and fruitful time of transformation. The author of the letter of Hebrews exhorted the early Christians when they faced their own crossroad. "Do not conform yourselves to this age but be transformed by the renewal of your mind, that you may discern what is the will of God, what is good and pleasing and perfect."[x] The crossroads are decisive. Two paths lie before us: the way of the world or the way of God. While we live with our feet in this world, faith informs our way of perceiving God, ourselves, and what's at stake in the choices we make.

Something beautiful happens when we permit the "fraternization" of God's grace and human collaboration. Little by little our new vision of reality informs the values to which we respond. Don't think it is easy. The formation of new habits is uncomfortable. Call it growing pains, from the old woman to the new. In the shedding, dying and leaving behind, nothing of one's essence is lost. One's true identity is merely refined. Mary likely experienced this, and despite future falls, a new strength to stand again is born. During this process, convictions take hold that enable a more determined and humble following of Christ. Let's watch and accompany Mary Magdalene as this dynamic unfolds in the next chapters.

Read Chapters 23-30.

Reflection & Sharing Questions (Part 5)

After Reading Chapters 23-30

SACRED SCRIPTURE

Take note of predominant scriptural passages that moved you. What word or phrase resonated more than any other? What predominant interior movements were provoked as you read them? Did you sense a strengthening in faith, hope or charity? Consider those passages as consoling and strengthening experiences. Return in prayer to those that strengthened you.

Scripture Passage	Phrase or Word	Interior Movements	Strengthening of faith, hope or love for God?

LIFE EXPERIENCES

Take note of any of Mary Magdalene's experiences, be they interior and emotional or exterior and historical, that moved you. How do you identify with her? What predominant memories and emotions from your own life were provoked?

Mary's experience	Interior Movements	Memories of my life

SPIRITUAL LIFE MAP

Use the Spiritual Life Map charts at the end of the *Companion* to take note of the PEOPLE & EVENTS in your life that have been important in shaping your faith journey. Continue to add to your list as you work your way through *Becoming Magdalene*.

QUESTIONS FOR JOURNALING OR SHARING

✓ Reflect on a time when you felt abandoned or rejected? What defense mechanisms manifested themselves? Do you recognize certain lies and accusatory voices that were predominant? Share this experience with Jesus and write the response Jesus he offers you.

✓ Reflect on a time you experienced the comfort of a spiritual friend? How did they accompany you? Have you been that friend for others?

✓ Reflect on a time when Jesus may have been asking you to wait patiently? How did you live it? What helped? What didn't help?

✓ Prepare a confession to Jesus as a means of also professing your faith in his goodness and mercy.

TAKE TIME TO PRAY!

The following prayer exercise may help you to continue the spiritual dynamic of the Second Week.[xi]

♥ Invite the Holy Spirit into your prayer. Make an act of faith and trust that the Lord is present and that He desires to be with you. Pray: Lord God, grant that all my intentions, actions and operations may be directed purely to the service and praise of Your Divine Majesty.

♥ Contemplate the Incarnation of our Lord Jesus Christ. See, hear and reflect upon:

  ♥ The lost situation of mankind: Consider the blasphemy and chaos of a world without God and the chasm created by their disobedience, lack of trust, idolatry and rejection of their Maker.

  ♥ The "heart" of the Trinity, determined since all of eternity, to work its plan of Redemption: Consider the Three Divine Persons of the Trinity looking upon all of humankind and conversing. They determine, in their eternal love, that the second person of the Trinity, the Word and Son of the Father, would become flesh in human history, in order to save humankind.

  ♥ The good news and response of the humble: Consider the angel Gabriel sent to a humble virgin who has been chosen to be the Mother of the Savior of the world. Consider her heartfelt response.

♥ Listen to the movements of your heart as you contemplate this fundamental mystery of your salvation. Ask the Lord for the graces according to how you feel interiorly moved, so as to more fully know, love and follow the Him.

♥ Close with a heartfelt *Our Father,* learning from Mary Magdalene how to ponder and savor the Lord's own prayer.

PART SIX: Second Week (3)

Called to Genius

Charm is deceptive, and beauty is fleeting;
but a woman who fears the LORD is to be praised.
Give her the reward she has earned,
and let her works bring her praise at the city gate.
Proverbs 31:30-31

Corresponds to Chapters 31-38

Spiritual Exercises' Dynamic (Part 6)
Second Week (3)

Read before Becoming Magdalene (Chapter 31-38)

Mary has begun accompanying the Lord. She has come face to face with her failings and shortcomings, but she has also tasted the joy of intentionally living for Jesus. Blessed friendships, reconciled relationships, attentive and heartfelt prayer, memories of her times with Jesus, and her humble confession have forged a deeper conviction to continue following him, aware of her own weaknesses.

Her friendship with Jesus is unique, as is ours. It has a "heart quality" about it, beating stronger and livelier as we fall more in love with him. But this requires truly encountering him. Watching, observing, not from the outside, but from the inside. We begin to wonder what he thinks, what he feels, how he loves. This is called contemplation. We begin to feel *for* him and *with* him. Mary had the privilege of an encounter with the living, breathing Jesus. We also have that privilege, through grace, and specifically in prayer.

Prayer, as Saint Teresa of Avila stressed, is about a relationship, about friendship. It leads to a loving encounter by which the Spirit gives birth to virtues. The grace of God waters the garden, causing the flowers to grow. The thorns are trimmed and blossoms give off fragrance, glorifying God. These flowers are offered to Jesus in loving service and charity toward all.

Prayer is a necessary condition for a disciple of Christ. By it, the heart is transformed into disciples that love more purely. It is not a transformation that changes the person into someone else. Rather, the person becomes more fully themselves in all their gifts now offered to the Lord. Let's watch as this transformation continues in Mary as she exercises her feminine genius, contributing something beautiful to Jesus' salvific mission by her very way of being woman.

Read Chapters 31-38.

Reflection & Sharing Questions (Part 6)

After Reading Chapters 31-38

SACRED SCRIPTURE

Take note of predominant scriptural passages that moved you. What word or phrase resonated more than any other? What predominant interior movements were provoked as you read them? Did you sense a strengthening in faith, hope or charity? Consider those passages as consoling and strengthening experiences. Return in prayer to those that strengthened you.

Scripture Passage	Phrase or Word	Interior Movements	Strengthening of faith, hope or love for God?

LIFE EXPERIENCES

Take note of any of Mary Magdalene's experiences, be they interior and emotional or exterior and historical, that moved you. How do you identify with her? What predominant memories and emotions from your own life were provoked?

Mary's experience	Interior Movements	Memories of my life

SPIRITUAL LIFE MAP

Use the Spiritual Life Map charts at the end of the *Companion* to take note of the PEOPLE & EVENTS in your life that have been important in shaping your faith journey. Do you notice moments of consolation when your faith, hope or love were strengthened, even in periods of dryness, sorrow or confusion? Continue to add to your list as you work your way through *Becoming Magdalene*.

QUESTIONS FOR JOURNALING OR SHARING

✓ Reflect on how you possess the "Martha" and "Mary" tension in your own heart. Do you recognize the need to "be at the feet of Jesus"? How and when can you make that happen?

✓ Reflect on your primary relationships and your attitude of the heart towards each person. Is there any aspect of un-forgiveness that you would like to pray about, ask strength to overcome?

TAKE TIME TO PRAY!

The following prayer exercises are part of the spiritual dynamic of the Second Week.[xii]

♥ Invite the Holy Spirit into your prayer. Make an act of faith and trust that the Lord is present and that He desires to be with you. Pray: Lord God, grant that all my intentions, actions and operations may be directed purely to the service and praise of Your Divine Majesty.

♥ Contemplate any of the following mysteries of Jesus' life. Use your imagination and memory to recall the mystery and enter into the time and place with your "spiritual senses". The corresponding scripture passages may also be helpful. In this "composition of place", look, listen, smell, taste, touch. Ponder whatever strikes you about Jesus and his personal love for you. End with a heartfelt colloquy and an Our Father.

> ➤ Mary and Joseph's long and uncertain journey from Nazareth to Bethlehem
> ➤ The Nativity in a humble cave of Bethlehem in the dark and cold of night (Luke 2:1-20)
> ➤ The presentation of Jesus in the Temple (Luke 2:22-40)
> ➤ The flight into Egypt (Matthew 2:13-23)
> ➤ The finding of Jesus teaching in the Temple at the age of twelve (Luke 2:41-52)
> ➤ The healing of the young boy at the foot of Mount Tabor (Matthew 17:14-22)
> ➤ The raising of Lazarus from the dead (John 11:17-46)

PART SEVEN: Second Week (4)

Called to Trust

Trust in the Lord with all your heart
and lean not on your own understanding;
in all your ways submit to him,
and he will make your paths straight.
Proverbs 3:5-6

Corresponds to Chapters 39-44

Spiritual Exercises' Dynamic (Part 7)
Second Week (4)

Read before Becoming Magdalene (Chapter 39-44)

Mary's depth of knowledge of herself has grown alongside a depth of knowledge of Christ. We have witnessed her reconciliation with God, with Martha and Lazarus, and she has made steps toward peace with various wounds of her past. This has freed her to follow Jesus with greater consciousness of both her weaknesses and gifts. It has freed her to love more fully and value the gifts that each of Jesus' followers offer. She has sincerely received counsel, and even corrections, from others and striven to be obedient to the Lord's invitations as well as his desires. Convictions have taken root. But they will be tested and solidified further in the months ahead. She is forming the heart of an authentic disciple with her unique qualities, gifts and her feminine genius.

We skip ahead one year in her story. Jesus' final Passover is approaching. The culmination of his salvific hour is upon us. As the time draws near, a new invitation emerges: to trust in God's Providence despite the shadow of the cross. She and the other disciples will wrestle with the inevitable. Like Mary, the joy of walking with the Lord increases our love and desire to serve him. But it always follows the pattern of his own life. His disciples are drawn into the mystery of suffering where the heart is further purified. The same sentiments of Christ are being formed within the depth of the disciple.

As we follow Jesus we may discern his call to a more defined and particular vocation such as marriage, chastity for the sake of the kingdom, missionary work, or the living of evangelical poverty, chastity or obedience in whatever state of life. It is a time of reflection, listening, discernment, decision and firm election. Making that election does not imply one has achieved the final goal. It is, nonetheless, a firm stance in professing one's faith and determination to follow the Lord in a particular and discerned way.

The election is made. One step is taken. At times, we cannot see beyond the first step into the darkness. Or we see only the hand of Jesus, reaching out and inviting trust. Whatever the call, a fundamental disposition is required. Courage! Trust and surrender to the Lord, in the mystery of darkness, must prevail. Trust that Jesus will provide the oil for our lamp. Thus, he illuminates that one next space before us. And if courage does not fail us, we step in.

Read Chapters 39-44.

Reflection & Sharing Questions (Part 7)
After Reading Chapters 39-44

SACRED SCRIPTURE

Take note of predominant scriptural passages that moved you. What word or phrase resonated more than any other? What predominant interior movements were provoked as you read them? Did you sense a strengthening in faith, hope or charity? Consider those passages as consoling and strengthening experiences. Return in prayer to those that strengthened you.

Scripture Passage	Phrase or Word	Interior Movements	Strengthening of faith, hope or love for God?

LIFE EXPERIENCES

Take note of any of Mary Magdalene's experiences, be they interior and emotional or exterior and historical, that moved you. How do you identify with her? What predominant memories and emotions from your own life were provoked?

Mary's experience	Interior Movements	Memories of my life

SPIRITUAL LIFE MAP

Use the Spiritual Life Map charts at the end of the *Companion* to take note of the PEOPLE & EVENTS in your life that have been important in shaping your faith journey. Do you notice moments of consolation when your faith, hope or love were strengthened? Or temptations to desolation, away from faith, hope and love? Do you recognize his call to friendship, deeper conviction of his love, and trust? Continue to add to your list as you work your way through *Becoming Magdalene.*

QUESTIONS FOR JOURNALING OR SHARING

✓ Where do you sense God's providence at work in your present life challenges?

✓ Where do you feel that you most need to trust in the midst of uncertainty and suffering?

✓ How can you, like Mary, keep your "lamp lit" so you can cultivate a loving and reverent heart toward the Lord?

TAKE TIME TO PRAY!

Saint Ignatius bookmarks the Second Week with "The Call of the Eternal King" and an election to follow Christ more radically. This call and response dynamic is facilitated by contemplating the Lord's loving obedience to the Father's will in poverty, humility and service. The retreatant contemplates his Incarnation, infancy, adolescence, the beginnings of his public ministry, his calling of the disciples, teachings and healings and finally his triumphant kingly entry into Jerusalem. Entering into these mysteries, the retreatant listens to the call of Christ, their King in the depth of their own heart. They allow themselves to be attracted by the Lord in his poverty, humility and loving service. They are drawn into knowing, loving and desiring to leave behind what holds back a greater following of the Lord.

Nestled in the midst of these contemplations are two meditations to prepare the retreatant to make "an election". The "Two Standards" opens a path to discern the difference between the enemy's versus Christ's invitations.xiii The enemy's false invitation is manifest in the temptations of honor, pride, and other vices. The Lord's invitation is one that leads to greater service and praise of the true Lord, but requires a spirit of poverty and humility.

The second meditation is call the "Three Kinds of Men".xiv It returns to the principle and foundation to examine the state of spiritual indifference one has toward Jesus' call. Ignatian indifference requires a disposition of openness to the Lord, free of the heart's graspings onto false idols. Without it, our discernment is often clouded due to the influence of the evil spirit's subtle temptations and/or our own subconscious psychological mechanisms.

Finally, before making the election or reform of life, Ignatius recommends considering "Three Degrees of Humility". In Mary's walk through the desert and conversations with John and Matthew, they reflected on the different ways in which people have responded to the Lord's invitation, including their own. Some responded with obedience to God's ten commandments and nothing more. Another simply chose to follow, not regarding if it meant being rich or poor. According to Ignatius, the third way of humility, the most radical, is to choose the way of Christ: that of poverty, persecution and to be considered a "fool for Christ".

Take time, like Mary Magdalene, to "retreat" to the desert. Consider how you have experienced the Lord's invitations to follow him. Examine your heart. Where does it seek self-glorification? Where does it seeks, in all things, to praise and glorify the Lord? Walk with him and speak with him about how he desires you to respond and ask for the graces you most need to love with a pure heart. End with a heartfelt colloquy of praise and adoration.

CONCLUSION TO Second Week
New Life in Christ

New life in Christ is exciting, but wrought with provocations. We are still the same person, yet different with God's sanctifying grace. Jesus warned, "don't pour new wine into old wineskins."[xv] God cannot be contained in our old skin, so to speak. He is utterly new. While it is true that He comes to us where we are at, He doesn't permit us to remain the same. He sees the whole of us, weak and potentially holy. As we befriend him, the temptation exists to fit Jesus into our past schemes. What a revelation to discover that "he simply is what He is, so utterly new, unique, that He can only be approached and accepted on his terms."[xvi] Hence, the crossroads that so many have faced through the centuries - to leave behind their riches, leave off burying their dead, leave family, all for the sake of following Jesus.

We arrive at the crossroads daily. And it provokes necessary transformation. More than forgoing tangible goods, Jesus invites us to leave something of our old self behind, letting it die so as to experience a new freedom. Some discomfort is inevitable. Like embarking upon a physical fitness program or learning to play piano, our heart is in the right place, but the muscles are not familiar with the new movements. They don't come naturally, not yet anyways. It is rough going and at times painful while everything strengthens and muscle memory develops. So it is in our journey with the Lord. Our spiritual muscles may be flabby, weak, and not accustomed to certain habits.

Despite Mary Magdalene's seven demons, she must have been a noble soul – someone capable of responding from the heart. The natural law was written within her, as it is in us. We possess a "sixth sense", so to speak, helping us perceive right and wrong, what is good and noble, if we are sincere and listen carefully. Whether we follow through on the inclination is another story. Like Mary Magdalene, following Jesus appeals to the innate noble self. We set out with initial zeal to follow the Lord. Suddenly, we are surprised to discover more powerful proclivities. Lingering echoes of previous tendencies resurface. They aren't willing to easily admit defeat. Pride tempts a hungry ego, vanity cries out to preserve its image, and self-indulgence demands to be fed. But the Lord still invites us to follow him. And thank God, He is willing and available to walk with us at every step.

Will we let Him? Will we discover we are loved and allow ourselves to be moved to reverence, adoration and selfless gestures of love for him? Will we follow him, even when it implies a journey to Calvary? Mary did. And that gives us hope. Her love for Jesus blossomed into that of a bride for the bridegroom. Now it will be forged and purified in the crucible of suffering.

PART EIGHT: Third Week

Called to Fidelity

Remember that you were at that time separated from Christ,
alienated from the commonwealth of Israel
and strangers to the covenants of promise,
having no hope and without God in the world.
But now in Christ Jesus
you who once were far off
have been brought near by the blood of Christ.
Ephesians 2 12-13

Corresponds to Chapters 45-50

Spiritual Exercises' Dynamic (Part 8)
Third Week

Read before Becoming Magdalene (Chapter 45-50)

On the first Holy Saturday, Mary Magdalene contemplates the mysteries of Jesus' sacrificial and redemptive offering. She awaits the great event of encountering the Risen Lord, albeit unknown to her. Her faith and trust are put to the test and strengthened through this dark night. Her love is forged in the crucible as she relives, in her memory, the previous hours of Jesus' passion.

In the third week we accompany Jesus in his redemptive passion in solidarity with the other women. Go with Mary to the rooftop of the Cenacle, the place of the Upper room, where she takes refuge after anointing the body of Jesus on Friday. There she contemplates all she had witnessed until she is able to return to the tomb early Sunday morning. She did not have the hindsight as we now have. In those long hours, upon the rooftop on Mount Zion, on the highest peak overlooking the holy city of Jerusalem, she has a view of the Mount of Olives and the Temple, and she knows the nearby direction of Golgotha. There she awaits the end of the Sabbath with the hope of reuniting with her beloved Rabboni.

It is a blessed time. It is a painful time. Memories usher the past into the present where wounds bleed anew, sight takes on a new perspective and mystery awakens awe. Her heart and mind are full of the echoes of the history of her people, God's liberating fidelity, her lived experience of her faith traditions, the expectancy of a Messiah, and her own knowledge of Jesus and his teachings. Things begin to fall into place. She is an astute woman. Hope is nurtured. But the revealed promise remains obscured by confusion and agony of having lost her beloved.

In St Ignatius' spiritual exercises we are invited to enter into the mystery of Christ's passion, as Mary did. We are no longer mere followers. We contemplate in solidarity with his sacrificial and salvific love. Our faith, hope, and love are strengthened as we learn how to be faithful at the foot of the cross. We contemplate Jesus' passion in light of his triumph over sin and death. We praise and give thanks to God for his tremendous, personal and universal love. We ask for perseverance and listen for the Lord's gentle response as we sing out, "How O Lord, can I return the favors you have poured out on me in your merciful love?" And we await in eager anticipation for the gift of his triumphant presence to come.

Read Chapters 45-50.

Reflection & Prayer (Part 8)

After Reading Chapters 45-50

SACRED SCRIPTURE

Take note of predominant scriptural passages that moved you. What word or phrase resonated more than any other? What predominant interior movements were provoked as you read them? Did you sense a strengthening in faith, hope or charity? Consider those passages as consoling and strengthening experiences. Return in prayer to those that strengthened you.

Scripture Passage	Phrase or Word	Interior Movements	Strengthening of faith, hope or love for God?

LIFE EXPERIENCES

Take note of any of Mary Magdalene's experiences, be they interior and emotional or exterior and historical, that moved you. How do you identify with her? What predominant memories and emotions from your own life were provoked?

Mary's experience	Interior Movements	Memories of my life

SPIRITUAL LIFE MAP

Use the Spiritual Life Map charts at the end of the *Companion* to take note of the PEOPLE & EVENTS in your life that have been important in shaping your faith journey. Do you notice moments of consolation when your faith, hope or love were strengthened, even in periods of suffering? Continue to add to your list as you work your way through *Becoming Magdalene*.

QUESTIONS FOR JOURNALING OR SHARING

Write a prayer to the Lord expressing your present sufferings and challenges. Place them at the foot of His Cross. Remember and receive the outpouring of his Sacred Blood shed out of love for you. Write your own psalm of praise, reverence and gratitude. How O Lord, can I return the favors you have poured out on me in your merciful love?

TAKE TIME TO PRAY!

Having made an election or a firm resolution to follow the Lord, the third week of spiritual exercises is a time to forge one's fidelity by taking up the cross. Enter into the mystery of Christ's sacrificial love for you. Take one of the moments that Mary Magdalene lived. Go there and stay with Jesus in solidarity with his sufferings. Contemplate the moment in sorrow and confusion, in heartfelt adoration and gratitude. See, hear, watch. Consider how his divinity was hidden as he took on the sufferings in the fullness of his humanity. Ask the Lord what you can do and suffer for him.

PART NINE: Fourth Week

Called to Discipleship

Since you call on a Father who judges each person's work impartially, live out your time as foreigners here in reverent fear. For you know that it was not with perishable things such as silver or gold that you were redeemed from the empty way of life handed down to you from your ancestors, 19 but with the precious blood of Christ, a lamb without blemish or defect. He was chosen before the creation of the world, but was revealed in these last times for your sake. Through him you believe in God, who raised him from the dead and glorified him, and so your faith and hope are in God.

1 Peter 1:17-21

Corresponds to Chapters 51-60

Spiritual Exercises' Dynamic (Part 9)
Fourth Week

Read before Becoming Magdalene (Chapter 51-60)

In the fourth week, the Paschal mystery culminates in the joy of Christ's Resurrection. We discover, with the disciples, the consolation of being strengthened in faith by the Risen Lord. Jesus convokes his Church, sending his Spirit to give them courage, wisdom, and the many necessary gifts to carry out his mandate. We, like Mary, are sent to proclaim the Good News, each to their own land, their own people, or to a new territory, depending on the unique and personal call of the Lord. As we contemplate the encounters with the Risen Lord, we too draw strength from him for our own lives. We are invited to say, "Send me Lord!" and listen for the nuances of our personal vocation as disciples of the Lord of life and history.

From the contemplation of these mysteries we, like Mary Magdalene and many other disciples of her day and throughout the ages, enter into the fullness of Christ's Paschal Mystery. More than a mere psychological identification, the Lord draws us into deeper friendship and discipleship. We come to share not only in the sufferings of Christ, but are co-participators in his redemptive work, which continues to be carried out on earth today. We discover what it means to be disciples as we experience ourselves uniquely and personally called. Within and from the heart of the Church, rooted in His Kingdom and established since the foundation of the world, we are sent to the ends of the earth to be His witnesses. May our testimony of joy, hope and charity be our first testimony of faith in the Risen Lord.

Read Chapters 51-60.

Reflection & Sharing Questions (Part 9)

After Reading Chapters 51-60

SACRED SCRIPTURE

Take note of predominant scriptural passages that moved you. What word or phrase resonated more than any other? What predominant interior movements were provoked as you read them? Did you sense a strengthening in faith, hope or charity? Consider those passages as consoling and strengthening experiences. Return in prayer to those that strengthened you.

Scripture Passage	Phrase or Word	Interior Movements	Strengthening of faith, hope or love for God?

LIFE EXPERIENCES

Take note of any of Mary Magdalene's experiences, be they interior and emotional or exterior and historical, that moved you. How do you identify with her? What predominant memories and emotions from your own life were provoked?

Mary's experience	Interior Movements	Memories of my life

SPIRITUAL LIFE MAP

Use the Spiritual Life Map charts at the end of the *Companion* to take note of the PEOPLE & EVENTS in your life that have been important in shaping your faith journey. Do you notice moments of consolation when your faith, hope or love were strengthened? When you desired to be the Lord's disciple? Continue to add to your list as you work your way through *Becoming Magdalene*.

FOR JOURNALING OR SHARING

- Make a list of the scriptural passages that presently echo in your heart as words spoken personally to you. How do they nurture your faith, hope, and love?
- Write a prayer of memory, sharing about and praising God for a time when you felt buoyed by hope, despite not understanding His ways.
- Make a list of people whom you would like to pray for, especially for an increase of faith. Bring them before the Lord.

TAKE TIME TO PRAY!

In the spiritual exercises of the Fourth Week, Ignatius recommends beginning at the empty tomb, as we did with Mary Magdalene, and moving into an encounter with the Risen Lord.

- ♥ Begin by invoking the Holy Spirit. Ask for the grace to rejoice in the presence of the Risen Lord.
- ♥ Begin in the "empty tomb", a void or space that is in search of life and the presence of your beloved Lord and Savior.
- ♥ See, hear, and reflect on the mystery of Jesus' Risen presence by using any of the following scenes.
    - ♥ Jesus appears to his mother Mary (This is an event maintained by tradition and assumed from the scripture passage 1 Cor. 15:6). It is the first meditation recommended by Saint Ignatius.)
    - ♥ Mary Magdalene's encounter with the Risen Lord in the garden (John 20:11-18)
    - ♥ Jesus appears to several women (Mt 28:8-10)
    - ♥ Jesus appears to Peter and to the disciples on the road to Emmaus (Lk 24:12-34)
    - ♥ Jesus appears in the midst of the disciples in the upper room (John 20:19-23)
    - ♥ Jesus appears to St Thomas (John 20:24-29)
    - ♥ The Ascension of Jesus (Acts 1:3-11)

PART TEN: Contemplation to Attain Love

Called to Union

He has saved us and called us to a holy life—
not because of anything we have done
but because of his own purpose and grace.
This grace was given us in Christ Jesus before the beginning of time,
but it has now been revealed through the appearing of our Savior,
Christ Jesus, who has destroyed death
and has brought life and immortality to light through the gospel.
And of this gospel I was appointed
a herald and an apostle and a teacher.
2 Timothy 1: 9-11

Corresponds to Epilogue

Spiritual Exercises' Dynamic (Part 10)
Contemplation to Attain Love

Read before the Epilogue

St Ignatius offers a final prayer exercise called the "Contemplation to attain love". Consider two fundamental aspects of our journey. First, that love manifests itself in works more than in words. Secondly, love consists in both receiving and giving. Therefore, turn your memory to the blessings received from creation, redemption and personal charisms and gifts received and developed throughout your life. Through the lens of faith, examine, meditate and contemplate the Lord's gifts as an expression of the gift of Himself, ordered to your salvific good. He loves you into eternity. In receiving His gifts, you receive, above all, his very person. In turn, you offer the gift back with a loving heart.

This dynamic of mutual exchange, in which God loves us first, invites a response on our part. In responding, we are taken up into union with the Lord's life and work, which is the life and mission of the Church itself. We will close our story by reflecting on Mary Magdalene's call to union through multiple forms of discipleship.

Our story left off shortly after Pentecost, a new beginning in the Church. We have yet to witness her continued adventures as one of Jesus' beloved disciples. Traditions abound. The first is prevalent in Eastern Orthodox churches. Within a few years after Jesus' crucifixion, she ventured to Rome where she confronted the Emperor about Pontius Pilate's unjust sentence of death upon Jesus. In her zeal, she gave witness to the good news. An egg miraculously turning the color red configures into the story. True story or not, we see in it her noble and passionate heart. She determines for herself how she will carry out the mission for the Lord. At the heart of this tradition is the seed of her gospel witness to Christ's resurrection.

The second tradition is popular in the Western church, particularly in the French Catholic church. One detects a development in her way of being a disciple in circumstances out of her control. Fourteen years after the resurrection, during a period of Christian persecution, Mary and several other disciples, including women acquaintances and her spiritual father Maximin, are abandoned at sea. They drift to the pagan land of Gaul, under Roman domination. The heart of her gospel witness shines forth in her preaching of the good news. Her intercession for the local leader's wife and child bears fruit in healing and conversion. Eventually she retires to a cave to live the life of a contemplative penitent.

The cave appears to be a death to this world, but echoes a unity of life with Christ. As St Paul expressed from his own heart, "For to me to live is Christ and to die is gain."[xvii] The cave symbolizes a total identification with the heart of Jesus in Mary's final desire for consummation and total oblation. Her complete self-offering, in bridal fashion, is an expression of unity with her bridegroom, which is also an identification with the mission of Christ and the mission of the Church. She is zealous for the eternal salvation of souls because "Christ's love compels" her. She, like St Paul, is "convinced that because one died for all…those who live should no longer live for themselves but for him who died for them and was raised again."[xviii]

Mary Magdalene's transforming life journey spiraled ever deeper in a process of learning to receive and give love. It is the life of every disciple. And it culminates when the Spirit and the Bridegroom say, "Come, my beloved!" Then we are awarded the final, yet eternal embrace of the Beloved.

As Mary's story comes to a close, look back on your own journey. If you have been adding to your spiritual life map as you accompanied Mary Magdalene, this is the time to take it up again. Or start it now. Using your theological memory, marvel at the blessings you have received and ask the Lord how you can return all the good he has done for you. Close in a prayer. You may like to use St Ignatius' famous prayer, *Take Lord*. In it, you express the desire to be taken up into a mutual exchange of loving union with the Lord.

Take, Lord, receive all my liberty, my memory, my understanding, my whole will, all that I have and all that I possess. You gave it all to me, Lord; I give it all back to you. Do with it as you will, according to your good pleasure. Give me your love and your grace; for with this I have all that I need.[xix]

Read the Epilogue.

Suggested Activity: Spiritual Life Map

Look back on your life journey. Can you recognize the promptings of the Lord in the midst of messiness, in the highs and lows of life? A helpful activity is to make an historical timeline or spiritual life map, noting important moments in your relationship with the Lord. Reflect on influential persons and events, positive or negative, that have influenced your faith journey. Pay attention to those in which you felt strengthened in faith, hope or love and those in which God seemed distant. Can you recognize His presence and promptings now, as you look back? Use the questions at the end to further your prayerful reflection and share with others.

Build your life map as you continue reading the story of Mary Magdalene. Perhaps her own experience will prompt memories of your relationship with the Lord. If you were to reread your life in the light of God's narrative, how he loves you and calls you to be part of His loving plan, what changes about your vision of God, yourself and your relationship with Him and others?

Use the charts below to reflect on the PEOPLE OR EVENTS in your life that have shaped your perception of your identity and purpose, and your perception of God.

Column A: Name the most influential people and the most impacting events in your life.

Column B: Name the predominant affective (emotional) movement that is provoked upon recalling the person or event. In other words, when you think of your interactions with them, how do they make you feel? "safe", "secure", "at home", loved unconditionally, or threatened, fearful, abandoned, etc. Or what is the predominant emotion you associate with that event?

Column C: Reflect on what beliefs or convictions related to your identity, purpose, belonging, or worth have been shaped and reinforced through that relationship or event. Then reflect on the same in your relationship with God. How has it influenced your relationship with the Lord?

A. Influential Person or Event	B. Predominant affective experience	C. Reinforced beliefs about God or self?

After you have filled in the influential people and events charts, take time to reflect.

- *How do you believe that God has strengthened or challenged you through that experience?*
- *How did you respond to that challenge?*
- *How does it affect you today? How has it made you who you are today?*

BE CREATIVE

Create a one page visual that reveals the various events, people and the Lord's presence and action. Use key words, images, dates, or whatever helps you to summarize God's narrative in your own life. Share this with a spiritual director or spiritual friend.

[i] Spiritual Exercises, no. 23.

[ii] The following incorporates parts of the first week's meditations in Spiritual Exercises, nos. 45-54.

[iii] Spiritual Exercises, no. 46.

[iv] John 10:10.

[v] Jeremiah 29:11.

[vi] Ps 8:4-10.

[vii] The following meditation echoes "The call of the temporal king to help contemplate the life of the Eternal King" in Spiritual Exercises, nos. 91-100.

[viii] Spiritual Exercises, no. 46.

[ix] Variation of the prayer St Ignatius offers in Spiritual Exercises, no. 98.

[x] Rm 12:2.

[xi] The following prayer echoes Saint Ignatius' contemplation on the Incarnation in Spiritual Exercises nos. 101-109.

[xii] Spiritual Exercises, nos. 110-163.

[xiii] Spiritual Exercises, nos. 136-148.

[xiv] Spiritual Exercises, nos. 149-157.

[xv] Mt 9:24.

[xvi] Fr Robert Presutti, May 1, 2020, personal email conversation.

[xvii] Philippians 1:21.

[xviii] 2 Cor. 5:14-15.

[xix] Spiritual exercises no. 234.

www.ingramcontent.com/pod-product-compliance
Lightning Source LLC
Chambersburg PA
CBHW081635040426
42449CB00014B/3321